PROPHECY
SEARCH FOR THE TRUTH

By: Jim Golden

Copyright Page

The material in this book is the copyrighted material of its author Jim Golden—DSMS and as such may not be reproduced in any medium for any purpose without the express written permission of the author.

© 2009 Jim Golden—DSMS • All rights reserved.

ADDITIONAL AVAILABLE BOOKS BY JIM (Also available in e-book format from www.lulu.com)

SIGNIFICANT LIVES

What is the GOSPEL of the Kingdom?

Counterfeit Christianity vs. the Kingdom of God

ISBN # 978-0-557-19469-8

PROPHECY—*Search For The Truth!*

This is the story of Jim Golden's life, and his search for meaning.

It is my prayer and hope that this book will encourage those who believe that their unsaved loved ones cannot be reached. With God, all things are possible!

TABLE OF CONTENTS

Chapter 1 - The Birth of a Prophecy

Chapter 2 - Big Bob & Bullets

Chapter 3 - Jimmy, Nelson & Colleen

Chapter 4 - Pneumonia, Rocks, & Quicksand

Chapter 5 - A Nickel & A Doughnut

Chapter 6 - Harleys, High School & Friends

Chapter 7 - Semper-Fi, Stigma of Shame

Chapter 8 - Dickey, Dee & Death

Chapter 9 - It's My Life, Let Me Live It Like I want Too!

Chapter 10 –A Date with Destiny

Chapter 11 —Jesus & Jail

Chapter 12 - Not Perfect, Just Forgiven!

The Birth of a Prophecy

Chapter 1

The year was 1948 and America was still learning to relax after the "Big One" WW-II. We had finally defeated Hitler, and watched Mussolini perish in the street. We dropped "Fat Man and Little Boy" on an unsuspecting Japanese Nation, and the taste of revenge lingered bittersweet on the palette of American society. Shouts of victory still danced with songs of joy in the hearts of many Americans.

It was July in Washington D.C. Like most summers there, it was hot and muggy. People still put blocks of ice in roasting pans. Setting them on their windowsills, they hoped to entice a fleeting summer breeze to cool itself, and share in the reward. I can still remember the 3-speed oscillating fan that would regularly substitute for the truant breezes of summer. Both reminded you of mother's old hair dryer, but some relief was better than none.

The Birth Of A Prophecy

It was July 2 and the first part of a prophecy was about to be fulfilled by a 19-year-old farm girl from Beltsville, Maryland. Some time earlier Doris Elizabeth had met a sailor named Bill Smith. Bill was what most church people would call an unlikely source of prophecy. During their short but passionate relationship, Bill told Doris something was going to happen to her that would changer her life forever.

Bill was what some might call a man with a prophetic gift. He prophesied to my mother before she even knew that she was pregnant that she would have a son. He would be born with white hair and grow up to be a preacher!

Bill Smith - Jim's alleged Biological Dad in 1948

Much of these days remain sketchy because of the lack of a family historian, but Doris and Bill never married.

PROPHECY — Search For The Truth

I was born with white hair and I was a boy. In fact my hair was so white that it earned me the family nickname of "Sonny."

Doris Elizabeth's father had died when she was very young, leaving her mother Betty to raise her and two sons alone. Betty was little more than a child herself, being only 13 when she gave birth to Doris. These two women were the original "emancipated" ladies of their day. Together they tackled the business of living head on. Everyone thought of them more as sisters than mother and daughter.

The war had ushered in a "new" era of morality. Mr. Smith's name could be found on the hotel and motel registers in every town and port of call in the world. The next few decades renamed this new morality the "Free Love" movement. Within its loins were the seeds of disease, destruction and decay. By the early 1990's America would be engaged in a dreadful war to preserve family sanctity and Christian values, the nucleus of its society. A war, the outcome of which is still not known!

Whatever is known about Bill Smith today is vague but there is one thing certain, he was a very handsome and charismatic man. Some old photographs depict him as a blonde, curly-haired sailor with a whimsical smile that might capture the affections of any young woman. Love has conquered kingdoms and wars have raged in its name. Doris' meager and fleeting attempts to withstand the onslaught of Bill's affection surrendered to a moment of foolishness. They soon became what Hollywood might call an "item."

The problem with being an "item" is that you're too much like a fad. Remember bell-bottoms? Fads come and go, and so did Bill, but he never came back; at least not yet.

Just how all these events would fit into the plan of God wasn't on Doris' mind that sultry day in July. She was learning for the first time how painful love can be. After a lengthy and difficult labor she saw the first part of the prophecy fulfilled. When the doctor's hand stung the bottom of her newborn, white-haired son, she listened to his first sounds of life.

Holding him close to her heart, she wondered if it were simply coincidence. "Doris, you're going to have a son who will be born with white hair. When he grows up he will become a preacher." As she lay on the hospital bed, the piercing words Bill had spoken moved through her thoughts like an ever-present, yet unseen specter.

The first two parts of the prophecy had already come true with little or no conscious effort on her part. As she looked into her son's eyes she thought proudly to herself, that no matter what the future might hold, this incredible moment would justify the cost. At that moment the future was all sunshine and roses.

The days ahead would watch sickness and calamity try to foil the fulfillment of the prophecy again and again. However, over the years Doris would come to realize that when God speaks it must come to pass. The vessel He uses is of little consequence. God's Word is a creative force. It is Spirit and life!

Big Bob and Bullets!

Chapter 2

"I can't help myself Betty. When I think of another man touching you or even talking to you I go crazy!" These were the repenting words "Big Bob" spoke to Betty just after he had beaten her policeman suitor to a pulp. Bob was normally a "gentle giant" but some secret demon or mysterious dark power rose to the surface when any man showed her the least bit of attention. It wasn't that he wanted to own her. It was beyond the realm of definition or explanation.

This scenario seemed to be a trigger that brought about some type of strange metamorphosis. Like his TV counterpart, Dr. Bruce Banner, Bob would change into an eerie creature filled with rage and super-human strength whenever he felt his relationship with Betty was threatened. However, this relationship was not a two way street, in Bob's mind, Betty was his.

Big Bob & Bullets!

Doris and her infant son were living in a small three room, second story apartment situated over a local "watering hole". It wasn't anything fancy but it was clean and the neighborhood wasn't that bad. It was a typical community in Washington D.C. in the late forties. Country music was still popular then and the city seemed to have a "country" small town flavor in that part of town.

It was getting close to suppertime when Bob exploded through the apartment door. Out of breath and turning quickly he slammed the door shut and threw the dead bolt to the locked position. Leaning with his back against the door he cried out for Betty. As she came running from the bedroom leaving Doris and Sonny, she noticed that Bob looked afraid for the first time since she had known him.

"Betty, just tell me you love me!" Bob gasped as he sought to recover his breath. "Bob, what's wrong? What have you done now?" "I can't believe I did it," Bob said. Betty could see a far away look come over Bob like some ghostly-unseen shadow, enshrouding him. "Bob, tell me what you did!" Terrified, Betty pleaded with him to leave when he said, "Betty, I just killed a cop!"

Doris, overhearing his confession joined with her mother in begging him to leave the apartment. "I have a baby in the other room, please leave." The glazed look in his eyes said it all. Like a big cat cornered by its keepers, he was desperately seeking an avenue of escape within his mind. He had determined, long ago, that he would never go to prison again. Suddenly an almost peaceful resolve came over him, as though his fate had been revealed to him. One thing was certain; they wouldn't take him back to jail again.

Deep down inside he knew it would never work out between him and Betty, especially now. He knew it was only a matter of minutes before the unavoidable knock would come at the door, followed by those familiar words, Police! Open up! What a perfect end to a miserable life. Maybe Betty would finally believe that he truly loved her. Maybe, at least, she would never forget him. He was going to lay his life down in front of her. Bob wasn't going to commit suicide; he still had four rounds left in his revolver.

"Get back into the bedroom Doris, he's got a gun," Betty pleaded. BAM, BAM, BAM, it was too late. Bob would never get to deliver his last mournful love sonnet to Betty. Betty would never get a chance to flee into the other room with her daughter and grandson. Doris would never get a chance to object to being treated like a child and told to hide in the bedroom. No sooner had the word "police" penetrated the apartment door than the last four cartridges in Bob's revolver spent their load, hurtling four chunks of hot lead through the door into the hallway, killing another policeman and wounding two more.

The apartment door literally disintegrated before their eyes as the deadly rain of police fire filled the air. Bob's hulking body seemed to be suspended in the air by some invisible force, as his already dead form was torn to shreds by "friendly fire". Today we call what Bob did "suicide by Police".

The funny thing about shock is the way it seems to protect us and get us through times of almost unimaginable horror. Shock is what Betty and Doris were in. The walls were riddled with bullet holes. Several rounds had penetrated the room were Doris and Sonny were. Two rounds splintered the headboard of Sonny's crib where only moments ago he lay. Fortunately Doris had instinctively grabbed him and covered him with her own body.

As mother and daughter looked at each other and realized that they were alive they began to shake almost simultaneously. Doris suddenly ran to the bathroom as the reality of what happened hit home with nauseating effect. After many hours of questions and answers, the last policeman said as he was leaving, "Sorry for the mess ma'am, we didn't know anyone else was in here."

Jimmy, Nelson & Colleen!

Chapter 3

After the dust began to settle and Bob had been buried we moved to a different part of town. The newspapers had begun to use their ink for other stories beside the jealous lover who killed the cops, and life was slowly returning to normal. You have to understand that the word "normal" is a relative term. What was normal for our family is infamous in some more "orthodox" or conservative homes. By the time I was 17 we had moved more times than I could remember and we were already on stepfather number four.

I don't remember much about my real father or my first two stepfathers. The man I was named after was a diesel mechanic. He worked for a large trucking company, rode Harley-Davidson motorcycles and loved pork barbecues and cold beer.

Jimmy, Nelson & Colleen

Doris and Jimmy seemed made for each other. The Dixie-Pig saw them laughing together on many summer nights. It was a local hangout that catered to "good old boy" bikers and played country music. It was a place to have a little innocent fun. "Innocent" is a relative term too. I was never quite sure why Jimmy and mom parted ways. I had not been born at the time of their separation as far as I know. I think he suspected that she might not be faithful to him. I never saw him again until I was twelve or thirteen.

Jimmy Sr. & Doris in 1948

I one thing I did inherit from Jimmy beside his name — was his love for Harley-Davidsons. The last I heard from him he still owned his original motorcycle, I believe he purchased in 1937. While he claims not to be my father I resemble him more than any of my other "fathers".

My next stepfather was a man named Nelson. He was a big switch from the kind of man my mother usually dated, or so the story goes. As I remember it, he was a lawyer. Shortly after Doris and Nelson were married, my mother brought home a little baby sister named Laura Colleen. She was a little bundle of strange sounds on the other side of the room. Something had changed upon her arrival, and I was no longer the center of the universe.

It was during this time in my life, 18 months old, that I began to develop future Marine Corps skills. One that I was particularly fond of developing was the grenade lob. During those days, Playtex hadn't invented the plastic bottle with the little collapsible bag. People still used solid glass bottles. I used these glass bottles that I used to develop my "lobbing arm". I had several targets, all designed to recapture the attention I had lost with the arrival of my baby sister. When all of them seemed to fail to achieve the desired result, only one option remained—eliminate the competition!

I would have succeeded if it weren't for those blasted handrails that kept objects out as well as they kept babies in. I do remember my failed attempts gaining me the recognition I so richly deserved. Somehow it wasn't quite what I had expected, though.

Jimmy, Nelson & Colleen

I remember even less about stepfather number two than I do about stepfather number one. Possibly because of the events that were about to take place. As the story goes, for no apparent reason Nelson burst into the apartment one afternoon and grabbed a pistol he had owned before he married Doris. Without a word he ran back out of the house. I never saw him again. It wasn't until years later that we were told that he was shot to death trying to rob a liquor store.

It is true that nobody ever promised us a rose garden, as the trite and hackneyed cliché goes. However, Doris had a knack for making me feel like a rose garden was just around the corner. One thing was certain; she had a flair for finding a new husband when an old one would leave. Enter stepfather number three. Joel was the first stepfather I have any real recollection of, but I don't want to get too far ahead in my story. I forgot to tell you that Colleen wasn't Nelson's child. When I was twelve I found out that she was Jimmy's little girl and that's why he came back around to visit. He didn't want anything to do with me; he was just being polite, hoping to be able to get his hands on Laura Colleen.

It is a shame my mother didn't let her go to be with him. Her life might have turned out differently. I am not sure, but I think it was her way of getting him back for not loving me as his own. I never got to talk with my mother about Colleen. It didn't seem to me that she loved her. Or if she did, it was a very small love by comparison to the love she had for me. I have always felt a little ashamed for being loved so much and Colleen so little. I do believe that she did end up with Jimmy and that her life ended up better than it was. Without God's grace and intervention, our unseen demons rule us all.

My memories are mine, and others might say that things were totally different. It seemed to me that Colleen lived a Cinderella existence without ever finding her prince. I was told that she was incorrigible and that because she had run away so many times she was being taken away from us and placed in a juvenile home. Some years later, after she was taken away, I saw her for about an hour at some court hearing where I was told she had turned into a prostitute and hated us. We never spoke and to this day I have never seen her again.

Jimmy, Nelson & Colleen

I am sure that I will never be able to say that I lived a life without any regrets. Who can? Some of the events that shape our live are beyond our control and others we could have changed. In either case, I regret never having known my sister. We are both still alive and maybe this is not the end of the story.

Pneumonia, Rocks, & Quicksand!

Chapter 4

When I was growing up, I had pneumonia the first six years of my life. It was a perennial visitor that blossomed around Christmas time every year, lasting well into the New Year. It often produced the fragrance of worry in my mother. I was considered a sickly child. This may explain the reason for what I perceived to be maternal partiality in my favor.

In later years, before my mother's home call, she told me she thought I would never live to fulfill the call of God on my life. Six years of pneumonia, compounded by tonsillitis almost succeeded in killing me. Remember Roy Rogers, the Lone Ranger and his faithful Indian companion Tonto? Well I wanted to be all three all at once. Shortly after an operation to

Pneumonia, Rocks & Quicksand

remove a pair of highly inflamed tonsils, it happened. While trying to recreate an episode on TV in my living room I fell down a flight of stairs with a rubber-tipped arrow in my mouth. The kind you could shoot at the TV. Set without danger o damage.

My eyes opened in the hospital room with the doctors embarking on what I later considered a highly dubious event. I will never forget the next hour of my life. I had to remain awake while they inserted all kinds of shiny things down my throat. None of them tasted like ice cream nor were they as comforting. My only preparation for this operation was the serious look on one doctors face, accompanied by the words, "Sonny, you're going to have to be a very brave boy." Brave had nothing to do with it. I couldn't have run if I had wanted to. Four large nurses and my own *traitorous* mother held me down trying to comfort me with one-liners like, "It won't hurt for very long."

You have to listen for key words in life like, "pain" or "hurt". When you hear them it's best to take them as a cue to exit as soon as possible. In this case the pain brought by the Doctors saved my life as I was severely hemorrhaging.

As I recall I switched to cartoons after that. In fact my life in general settled down to a rather calming pace. We were getting ready for another move and I would have to adjust to another new school at the end of the summer.

"4995 East Capitol Street S.E. Washington D.C." I said. "Very good Sonny, now say it again," Doris said firmly. "Awe do I have to" I said as I squirmed around in the kitchen chair? I was quickly recovering from the recent operation and move. Looking out the kitchen window I could see the woods our backyard bordered on. Therein lay a world of magic and adventure. "Yes you have to say it again; this is a new neighborhood and school. You must know where you live in case you get lost." "But mom, that doesn't make sense. If I know where I live how can I get lost?" I wined. "**Sonny**," the look in her eye and the tone in her voice suggested that I had sufficiently tested my boundaries. "Just say it again!"

The summer was passing slowly and the woods became a more than adequate substitute for the blacktop playgrounds and alleys I had grown up with. I would spend hours pretending I was Daniel Boone or some other famous frontiersman embarking on a mapping expedition for the President or some wonderful adventure in the wilderness. Unfortunately, scoundrels often hide in the wilderness seeking easy prey.

"My God, what happened to you?" my Uncle Kenneth demanded. "I was playing by the old bridge in the woods and some big boys threw rocks at me." "Quick show me where!" "Oh no you don't Kenneth, the boy is bleeding. Come here Sonny!" Doris said. Kenneth was mom's little brother but he was more like a big brother than an uncle to me.

Intent on revenge Kenneth darted out the door like a hungry wolf on a blood-trail. I was so proud I could burst when I saw him come out of the woods dragging the two rather frazzled and tattered culprits. It seemed as though they had already had a good thrashing and now insult was being added to injury. "Go on tell him you're sorry or I'll bust you again." Kenneth looked menacing as he let the words snarl from his mouth in his best "wise guy" imitation. A narrowing of his eyes and a tightening of his grip quickly produced a whimpering apology. One sharp kick in the rear followed by an admonition never to repeat such as act of hostility launched them on their way.

The summer I had thought would never end did just that all too quickly. Looming before me like a giant chasm was the terrifying entity known as "school". "But mom I don't feel too good." "You're okay Sonny, it's just the first day of school jitters," Doris explained. We had rehearsed the walk from the house to the bus stop many times. It was only a short distance from the house. From the front sidewalk my mother could watch my trek to the corner. I never knew a city block could seem like a country mile until that first day in the first grade.

Mud puddles, for me, held a mysterious attraction. They had an incredible ability to relieve stress, something I was beginning to feel as I approached a rather large crowd of unfamiliar children waiting for the bus. I imagined the boys my uncle had recently educated in the art of being friendly lurking in the crowd waiting to pounce on me. To lessen the tension I decided to jump over the mud puddle near the woods before joining the crowd.

Pneumonia, Rocks & Quicksand

Much of Washington was built on a swamp. In 1954 it was still possible to encounter quicksand. We lived in a neighborhood developed in just such an area. What is it about six year old children and mud puddles? I don't know of one child of six that goes out of their way to avoid one. In this sense I was an extremely normal child.

By the time I realized my mistake it was too late. This was no ordinary mud puddle. It was quicksand! The more I struggled the deeper it pulled me into its unrelenting depths. Just in the nick of time a very brave little black girl, in her new school dress, jumped in and risked her life to save me. With the help of some other children we were both soon pulled to safety.

To this day I don't know who that little girl is but if she reads this book and remembers saving a sickly little white boy from quicksand at a bus stop in Washington D.C. I hope she will drop me a line. As we grow older many of the things that happen to us seem like a book we've read or a movie we saw while others remain as vivid as the day they were lived. This is one!

A Nickel & A Doughnut!

Chapter 5

It was a beautiful spring day. It was the kind of a day that made living in a humid region worthwhile. Still cool from the departing winter, the fragrance of lilacs and lilies of the valley filled the air. It was a most difficult time to be a grammar school student. My already short attention span was reduced even more by the possibility of some great outdoor quest. The explorer's heart beating within me could not be stilled. The entire world was made of the material used by fruitful imaginations to create great adventures.

The back porch of our new house on Montello Avenue became the deck of a great pirate ship from which I surveyed the kingdoms I was destined to conquer. The alley behind my house became the pathway leading to the city of the evil king whose realm I had just overthrown. At its end, my coronation as the new wise and merciful benefactor awaited. Young men

A Nickel & A Doughnut

bowed and beautiful maidens curtsied as they sang my praises.

"Sonny, SONNY, where is your mind boy? I've been calling you for five minutes." "I don't know mom," I said. "I was just pretending..." "Never mind that now," Doris said. "I need you to do something very important for me." "What mom: I can do it, I can do it. What is it?" I shouted. "I want you to take this note and this money, don't lose it, and go to the store at the bottom of the hill. Give the note to the man in the store and bring me back the change and what he gives you." "O.K. mom, I can do it. You can count on me."

Unbelievable she was going to let me go on a real adventure! I had never been allowed out of the yard without an adult before. Now I was actually being given not only liberty but also an assignment. It was like being a secret agent or some important courier on a royal mission. Setting my face like flint towards the store I let nothing deter me. Entering the store I quickly found the man behind the counter and gave him the communiqué I was entrusted with.

Peering over the top of his spectacles his scrutinizing gaze made me feel a little uncomfortable. "You sure your momma wrote this note boy?" "Yes sir," I said, quickly holding out my hand for the package he was about to give me. "From now on tell her to call before she sends you to buy cigarettes. I can get into trouble for selling them to a minor." His voice had softened as he reluctantly handed me the package of KOOL filtered king size cigarettes.

I looked inside the bag to see just what had aroused such concern in this big man. Inside the bag, I saw the three packs of cigarettes a dime, a nickel and a penny. Suddenly the overwhelming aroma of freshly baked gloriously glazed doughnuts filled my nostrils. I became fatigued from my mission. The pain of hunger began to cloud my mind and rack my body. I was almost overcome by nausea due to hunger. Slowly I reached into the bag, pulled out a nickel and said, "Mister, give me a glazed doughnut please."

Outside in the alley, kneeling against the back of the store I slowly consumed my recently acquired reward. It was truly a culinary delight. A glazed doughnut ranked in the same category with a bag of peanuts and a trip to the zoo. This one was even better

A Nickel & A Doughnut

because I didn't have to ask for it. I bought it all by myself. As I languished in the aftermath of my feast a strange unseen voice I had never heard before began to speak to me. In later years I came to know this voice as my conscience.

This voice began to tell me that the nickel wasn't mine and I had stolen from my mother. Not only wasn't the nickel mine but I was never supposed to eat anything that wasn't given to me by my mother.

No matter how slow I walked or how much I meandered, the walk back up the alley to my house ended much too quickly. What was I to do? What would she think? Wait a minute; she might not say a thing. If she did I could just say I didn't know where the nickel was.

With my sweetest smile I opened the creaking back door and slowly entered the screened in back porch. "Mom, I'm home." Placing the package on the kitchen table I broke the land speed record from the kitchen table to the sand box. Trying to look like you are having fun when you are miserable is a learned skill that few six year old children naturally posses.

"Sonny I am so proud of you. Did the man at the store say anything to you?" In my most cheerful voice I said, "Yes mom, he said he could get into trouble for selling me cigarettes and that you should call him next time." "Is that all he said?" Then before I could answer, a radar look came over my mother's face. Somehow, I knew she knew that I knew she knew something was wrong. "What's wrong Sonny?" "Nothing mom," I said.

She was holding the bag in her hand and for some reason she began to inspect it. "What's that sticky stuff on the bag?" "I don't know," I said sheepishly. Why is it, when we know the jig is up we keep on dancing? Looking inside the bag she pulled out a slip of white paper. After a quick glance she said, "Sonny there is a nickel missing, where is it?" "I don't know," I said.

Similar to the first time I ever jumped off the diving rocks at Great Falls, I knew I had made a mistake I could never correct. With my arms and legs flailing wildly I wished desperately that I could reconsider my decision to jump. As the last words dribbled down my chin, I wished that I could turn back time and do it all over again. "Tell me the truth," she said.

A Nickel & A Doughnut

I don't think a more wretched six year old ever lived on Montello Avenue or on planet earth for that matter. My mother's probing patience and Sherlock Holmes' type inquiries soon got to the bottom of things. I think the traces of glazed topping on my upper lip and a call to the corner store were prime factors in solving the case. Even with my sorrowful confession and my mother's assurance that I was forgiven I never felt quite as trustworthy again.

Harleys, High School & Friends!

Chapter 6

Outside of being the class bully in the 5th grade and getting beat up my first week in the 7th grade most of my grammar school experience was uneventful. Once there was a great deal of excitement over a boy who contracted some form of meningitis and everyone in the school had to get inoculated. Apart from the measles, mumps, chicken pocks and Becky Sue I have very few vivid memories.

Just as I was graduating from 6th grade, I remember finding out that my "father" was coming to visit. I had not found out yet that Bill Smith was my biological father and still thought Jimmy was. I am still not sure who's who. It was an exciting day on Claggett Drive as the big 1200cc, "knucklehead" **Harley-Davidson** motorcycle pulled to the curb. As the big man with the brimmed Harley cap dismounted his iron steed I proudly thought, this is my dad.

I can still remember the rides he took me on, and how he came back later in his car and took me and my sister Colleen to visit with him and his new wife in Richmond. Once he even took me for a ride in a big rig. That's the kind of truck that pulls those long trailers you see on the highway all the time. He was a mechanic and had to rescue one of his company's drivers with a broken down truck hauling a load of perishables. After he took us home I never heard from him again except once. It wasn't until my persistent nagging provoked my mother enough that she finally revealed the truth. He had only wanted to try and gain custody of Colleen, his real daughter.

Well, summer soon came to an end and the pain of his rejection of me was swallowed by the fear of the 7th grade. You actually had to take showers with other boys, and to be "cool" you might even have to kiss a girl. I wasn't very tall and for some reason never excelled in baseball or basketball. I did do rather well in football until my mother saw one of the boys on my team almost tear off his kneecap.

It's a mother's solemn duty to deprive her children of fun in life threatening situations like these. They gladly accept scorn; ridicule and rejection if it means their little offspring will be safe. It is very important that they live up to their peer's definition of a "good" mother. It is the last child, not the first that seems to help redefine these rigid standards set by the "good mothers of America" foundation. It helps to have a father who loves football around too. So gymnastics was the only sport left for me.

It was on the gymnastic team that I met Cynthia. God never intended Cynthia to be the one who taught me about the birds and the bees but she was. She was 14 and I had just turned 13 when, unknown to me, she asked my mother for my hand in marriage. I don't know if that had anything to do with us moving again but I never finished out the school year at Broome Jr. High. Beside Becky Sue, who I only took out once or twice and a crush I had on Maria D. from afar, my romantic portfolio never grew much in those days.

Oh, I should mention one thing; I did meet my first and best friend in the 7th grade. We were introduced in a fight in the hallway outside of print shop. The blows we traded seemed to cement years of

Harleys, High School & Friends!

friendship. His name was Tommy K. and I can't remember who won the fight. Our friendship lasted all through high school into our early adult life. It was a time for experimentation of the worst sort.

At sixteen, I was attending high school, enrolled in a vocational study program. I was maintaining a B average in academics and an A average in vocational studies. We, in the program, went to school a half-day and worked a regular job. The Glenmont ESSO gas station employed me for an average of 60 hours a week. I made one dollar per hour and that was a lot of money in those days.

Joel, my third stepfather, earned that title by the length of time he and my mother lived together. He was probably the closest thing I had to a real father, even though I hardly ever saw him. He was always driving his taxicab. Joel had established a friendship with an elderly woman, Mrs. F, who thought of him as a son. She had grown too old to drive and he had volunteered to help meet her transportation needs as often as he could, at no cost to her.

One day Mrs. F decided that the 1954, 2-tone, 4-door Chevy with only 16,000 original, one-owner miles, might be an exciting birthday present for Joel's 16-year-old stepson. Boy was she a good guesser; it was a high point in my life. This car launched me into the ranks of adulthood and the socially acceptable in one fell swoop. The only problem was my working 60 hours a week, partying and going to school did not fit into a 24-hour day and still allow me any sleep. Something had to go.

This short-lived period in my life held some of my fondest memories. What I did not know was Joel was on the way out and Charlie was on the way in. I had become so accustomed to the "changing of the guard" that I cannot even remember if I bothered to ask why, this time. This sudden upheaval, just when I thought things were working out coupled with homosexual advances from my best friend all but devastated me.

I made it into the beginning of the second semester of my senior year at Wheaton high school. By this time, I was drinking like a fish. My grades went down so fast it was like standing in an elevator on the 99th floor when the cable snaps.

Harleys, High School & Friends!

The "free-love" movement was beginning to blossom and Tommy and I were trying to take advantage of every opportunity to prove we were worthy members.

I have deliberately left out many sexual encounters that I deeply regret. I now know that sexual experimentation before marriage, especially at an early age, is emotionally destructive even if the damage does not appear for many years. It almost destroyed my ability to emote normally and drastically inhibited my ability to trust anyone fully. As you might imagine this could be stressful to a marriage and hinder the development of an intimate relationship with a wife or Savior.

As a 12th grader I left much to be desired. As I said, my mother was leaving stepfather number 3 and stepfather number 4 was moving in. My whole life was being turned upside down again. Charlie wasn't a bad guy for a 4th father. He was a former Marine and a hard worker. He wasn't much at being a father though he tried. He did convince my mother that my failing grades might be redeemed through a career in the Marine Corps. It might even make a man out of me. Therefore, at the tender age of 17, I enlisted in the Marines, but I do not want to get ahead of myself. I will talk more about my experience in the Corps in the next chapter.

Some people are groomed for success and others for failure. I will let you guess into what category I fit. You talk about stress and poor self-image. I could write a book or two on those subjects. Yet God is always there waiting for us to receive his unconditional love and acceptance. In later years I would grow to understand more fully how much a human life is worth, no matter how depraved it may appear. I came to realize my worth when I realized the price that was paid to redeem a wretch like me.

Semper-Fi, Stigma of Shame!

Chapter 7

Shame is a very illusive yet crippling affliction affecting many Americans of all ethnic groups, ages and genders. It is the cause of much of the dysfunction in our society today. When I was 17 years old, I was a senior in high school. It was the height of the Viet-Nam War and the patriotic spirit that gripped the hearts of many came over me. So I dropped out of school and enlisted in the U.S.M.C. I wanted to be in the best military service I could be in and to me that was the Corps. It was 1966 and I thought I was a man.

I had come from an extremely dysfunctional family background having never known my real father and at the time of my enlistment I was on my fourth step-father, who was a former Marine. I made it through boot camp at Parris Island, SC, Infantry Training Regiment (ITR) at Camp LeJune, NC and had just completed my MOS training as a heavy equipment operator when my life was about to change forever.

Semper-Fi, Bye Bye or Die!

This was probably the first time that my living situation would reveal the bitterness, resentment and anger for male authority figures that flowed like a tsunami in my life. I use the word tsunami because on the service a tsunami is barely noticeable at sea, but it is a raging unstoppable force in the ocean depths. This tsunami deep within my soul was about to come ashore in my life. I am not tying to excuse the choices that I made which resulted in a Bad Conduct Discharge (BCD) from the Marines, but to reveal what I have come to belief were the motivating factors that drove me like a slave-master. It is my hope that my testimony might spare some young man from taking a similar course of action in their lives.

It has taken me thirty plus years to come to grips with the choices that I made as teenager, choices that affects my life to this day. I did not realize the destructive power of shame. After my discharged in 1969, I tried to destroy my life through drug and alcohol abuse. I had all but lost any positive self-worth or image. Yet God had other plans for me and in 1972, He revealed His love for me. For the last 30 plus years I have tried to be faithful. Yet, still deep down inside I haven't been able to escape or be fully healed of the shame of my actions when I was in the Marine Corps.

Recently I felt as though the Lord was trying to get to the root of this so that I could finally experience His love as my heavenly Father. There has always seemed to be something holding me back from experiencing the joy that the Bible claims is one of the foundations of the Christian faith. I have lived in denial for over thirty years trying to shift the blame onto the Corps or just sweep it under the rug. God is relentless even though He is patient. He will not allow shame to exist in our lives forever because it keeps His sacrifice from being fully effective. It steals from those held in its crippling grip what Jesus suffered and died to give us, true freedom!

For me the first step was to stop making excuses for my actions, admit to myself that they were my fault, and take responsibility. The second step will be to stop beating myself up and to forgive myself. That is harder than it sounds. I have even thought of writing the Commandant of the Marine Corps and asking for his forgiveness, but I am not sure how that would go over. Perhaps he would be more understanding than I think, but regardless we need to swear to our own hurt. I violated my covenant with the Corps and that is not something to take lightly. Our God is a covenant God.

Semper-Fi, Bye Bye or Die!

I have needed to forgive my father's for the abandonment I experienced by them and to ask for God's grace to help me through this deep wounding of my soul so that my bitterness and disappointment would no longer defile those around me. I hold the Marine Corps in my prayers before God and pray that they would be protected in their efforts to defend our freedoms, freedoms that we so often take for granted. AMEN!

Dickey, Dee & Death!

Chapter 8

The era of Jesus Freaks, hippies and heads was upon us. It was at the beginning of this age when I met Dickey. Richard was his given name, a good-looking young man with delusions of grandeur. His charismatic personality and air of acceptance allowed him to espouse many to his court of admirers. Not really wanting to stay with Charlie and my mother after my release from the Marine Corps, I soon became a follower of Dickey. My association with him would open the door to a new stage in my life.

Gracy Slick was suggesting that we should feed our heads and not just our bodies. As I began to *"expand"* my mind I actually believed, my desire to feed other people's minds had nothing to do with greed. In the early days before the age of paranoia, it was easy to make *"good connections"*. I was able to get almost any quantity of *"acid"* (LSD) or pharmaceutical cocaine at very low prices whenever I wanted.

Dickey, Dee & Death

It wasn't until I heard Steppenwolf's The Pusher man that I even had a clue that what I was doing was wrong. Even then, we rationalized that if we were fair in our prices, generous in our quantities and connoisseurs in our quality of merchandise we didn't fit into the category of a *"pusher"*. In fact, we were risking our freedom to provide the material needed to fertilize and fuel the philosophy of a new world order. We were providing what the people wanted.

One thing that was in short supply was good marijuana or weed as we often called it. With the backing of a local construction company owner who was an under-cover convert of the *"movement"* Dickey and I left for regions unknown in his 1967 Camaro. The plan was to go to Acapulco, Mexico. We had a name or two and rejoiced at the thought of kilos for $135 apiece. *No stems, no seeds, nothing you don't need. "Acapulco Gold" is some bad _ _ _ weed.* I will let you fill in the blanks. Cheech & Chong's little chorus became the pursuit of our days and nights. *Weed* was the staple of our lives. We would begin and end our day with it. It was almost a bonding ritual among us.

Sayings like, *"dope will get you through times of no money better than money will get you through times of no dope,"* shaped our philosophy. From Mexico to California, Dickey and I shared everything until our failure to find a lucrative contact in Mexico revealed the true meaning of our association and we parted ways. Dickey found a new friend to polish his armor and I found Reb.

Reb was a good friend. He took me into his house and treated me like family. He was a biker and businessman all rolled into one. While he adopted most of the attitudes of "hippiedom", he was different. Reb drank a little bit and from time to time if he drank a little bit more than a little bit he might get high. That was the exception, not the rule.

In those days, I would get *"out there"* pretty far and Reb provided a non-condemning source of stability for my life. I was a big fellow and a biker at heart. By this time, I had begun to use barbiturates and could get very mean for a good cause. Reb managed an apartment building in the Valley and ran a modeling agency, which I helped him start. I had a lifestyle most men only dreamed about. I was his enforcer, at least in my mind. Reb and I developed a reputation as people you could trust. We made sure all our models were paid and did not have to do anything they did not want to do.

At one point, we had over 1300 models in the agency, doing everything from "*cheesecake*" to "*hard-core*" porn. Because of my position in the company, Reb allowed me to open a small sideline business with Bob R. Whenever a new model came in I could audition her across the street in our studio and take a $50.00 finder's fee for my trouble. However, the porn business needed some additional help and narcotics were the solution. Dee was one of my sources for "reds". She owed me and she owed me big.

The fear in Dee's eyes will remain in my memory as long as I live. I was a force to be reckoned with in my youth. Not only was I a recent graduate from the California penal system, but I was an outlaw biker with "juice". I had proven myself by beating someone nearly to death in a fight and maiming many others. Now, right in front of me was the source of many years of suffering and I found the dreams of revenge and rage that had fed me through much of my time in jail strangely waning in that moment of opportunity.

As I said Dee was one of my sources for "reds", one of three types of "barbs" that were popular on the streets in the early '70's. She had been dodging me because she had taken my money for a couple of jars of "reds" and went out the back door, so to speak. Some of my friends told me they knew where she was.

Sure enough, I found her the next day and "jacked" her up for the money or the "reds". As you might have guessed, she had neither. In fear for her life, she offered me, a few credit cards she claimed belonged to her new boyfriend. Her reasoning was if she didn't come through with the goods I could expose her pretense the next evening. It sounded good to me; after all, you cannot get "blood out of a turnip".

Some hope is better than none, so the next evening I showed up at the address on the "boyfriend's" license. Not seeing Dee anywhere, I began to snoop around. Peeking into one of the apartment windows, I saw her and her girlfriend. The next thing I knew the police were all over me. Trying to explain that I was there to see Dee, they relented momentarily.

Talk about being played for a sucker, I think I hold the world's record. When the police produced Dee and

Dickey, Dee & Death

her girlfriend to corroborate my story, I felt a little like Jesus on the night of his betrayal. "I have never seen this man before," she said coolly.

It seems as though the apartment next door to Dee had been robbed and with goods in hand, the Police had seized the culprit. My life was tied up for the next three years in one incident after another relating to that fateful night.

I spent months in jail waiting to go to trial. Charles Manson would walk by my cell on his way to court very often. I remember thinking to myself, "what a twerp." He always had such a friendly smile as though we were members of some kind of secret brotherhood. I finally made bail and skipped town the same day. After about a year, I was caught and copped a plea. After I did my time I was supposed to leave the state immediately upon my release, but I ran into an old "friend"—Dee!

As she begged and pleaded for her life, all hostility just left me. To this day, am not sure what was going on in the unseen realms, but I believe that even as an unbeliever God allowed me to taste his mercy and forgiveness for Dee. Suddenly I found myself forgiving her and simply asking her if she had any money she could help me with. She assured me she had a little, but she would have to go get it. As I let her go out that door, I was letting go of some evil presence that had controlled my life for so long.

Drugs and violence would remain a part of my life for a few more years, but my heart was never wed to them as it had been before that day. Before she came back with any money, the thought that she might come back with the police inspired me to attempt my journey home to Maryland with the resources I had in my pocket.

I don't remember much about the journey home except that there was this sense that my life was going to change. The next few years found me trying to resist this feeling through my activities in a notorious motorcycle gang, which for reasons of safety, (my own) shall not be named.

It was during these days that God began to enact his plan to bring me to his precious Son, Jesus. In the midst of my excessive depravity, I had hung onto some *archaic* value that a man should work for a living. At that time I was the manager of a small electronics company in Rockville, Maryland. This position came about through my association with Steve B., the owner. A personal friend and fellow member of the "movement" I spoke of earlier, we considered it an honor to wear the title of "freaks."

The company was growing and we needed to take on some new employees. Enter Scott and Karen, God's undercover agents in the war for the soul of yours truly, Jim Golden. As "fate" would have it, I was being evicted from an apartment I was living in, and Scott and Karen were looking for a place to live locally to eliminate their commute from West Virginia. They seemed like a very nice couple and were an asset to the company so I made them the offer. We soon found ourselves living together on Homewood Parkway in Kensington.

PCP was becoming a popular drug among the biker community and very lucrative as well. You could easily obtain or produce your own Hog tranquilizer. It became big business in the club, bringing in millions annually in just the chapter I was directly associated with. It was a very dangerous drug because it allowed you to function while, for all practical purposes, you were unconscious. I can remember leaving a party in Baltimore and not remembering anything until the beam from my motorcycle's headlight struck the garage door of my house in Kensington.

It was like madness began to sweep the area as fear and paranoia began to be the rule of the day. The president of the mother club had decided it was time for him to retire and felt that he could do that rather nicely with a few million dollars from the club's treasury. As a result my moment of testing had come. I had been given my first contract. A 30/30 rifle was given to me and I was told to kill him on sight. It was during an annual party when all the chapters show up that it was to take place.

The scenario went something like this. Every year there was something called a mandatory run. In a mandatory every member better show up on his motorcycle ready to party and renew old ties and commitments or risk "excommunication" from the club. This meant surrender of your "colors" and motorcycle to the club. After all, if you weren't going to ride with them, you weren't going to ride. Anyway, the intelligence reports said that the "old man" was going to show up for one of his "old ladies"

Dickey, Dee & Death

while the whole gang was out on one of its "runs". It was my task to eliminate him when he did.

As hundreds of motorcycles thundered down the long dirt road to the black-top adjacent to the farm, evening was settling on the 250-plus acre property. Rumor had it that there were more than just a few bodies buried in back of the barns. It was to be my task to add one more to the collection of the defeated enemies of the club. Knowing the mesmerizing power this man had exerted over his followers caused me to spend the night pacing the grounds in fear. Not only was he clever and ruthless, but he had two highly aggressive and well-trained Dobermans, dogs for which I held a high degree of respect. However, the dawn found the air filled with the thunder of the returning warriors and the night produced no victim for my 30/30.

A few deaths from the wars with a rival club in Virginia and the commission of the burglary of the business I managed, while high on PCP rounded out my year. My attempt at enjoying my ill-gotten gain ended up in my arrest in a hotel restaurant by Cook County Police. Awaiting extradition in the infamous facility known as the Cook County Jail, I watched an epileptic convulse himself to death in my cell because the guard thought he was faking. I decided to sign the extradition papers and return to Maryland for trial.

You may be wondering what became of Dickey, well I read in a newspaper that he was the victim of a gangland style killing. He was found shot to death in a motel room with a 16 year old girl. She had been shot twice and he had been shot seven times in the face and chest as I recall.

It's My Life Let Me Live It Like I Want Too!

Chapter 9

My focus began to change from the pressures of club life to the world around me. I was there when it started and now I was remembering once again what had originally got my attention.

Woodstock, love-ins, freaks & hippies, Haight & Ashbury, Timothy Leary, Led Zeppelin, Janis Joplin and Jimi Hendrix, those were the years of discovery. The air itself seemed to be alive with limitless excitement and endless possibility. All the dreams and expectations I had labored to fulfill had been put to death on the gallows of failure. The doorway to a *"new age"* was suddenly flung wide open, right in front of me.

You would've had to have been there and a part of it to know what I mean when I say it was like the dawning of a new age. It seemed as though a whole culture or race of people was born overnight. They lived in a kingdom of love, joy and peace. Many of the "old order" inhibitions and bigotries had drowned in a sea of *"Leary's elixir of love"*.

Slogans like, *"let LSD set you free,"* filled the thoughts of a war-weary generation of youth. They were tired of the "older" generation dictating to them the way they should live or think. Jimi Hendrix, a former Marine, now "reborn" acid-rock guitarist, and psychedelic Guru, championed the cause of this new freedom. A new outlook on life was birthed with lyrics like, "...nobody can die when it's time for me to die, it's my life, so let me live it like I want to."

There was a sincerity of love and acceptance many had only dreamed about. We were the counter-culture, a society within a society. We were a generation that was truly on a "magical mystery tour." No one knew where we would end up or where the road would take us and we did not care. We were the new existentialists, living our lives without regard for any future consequences, adopting a philosophy of, "if it feels good, how can it be wrong?" Still we were unwilling to take responsibility for our actions, yet we would eventually reap what we sowed.

I remember some of the struggles the Nation went through in its efforts to define pornography. At one point I had been in a partnership with a man named Bob R. We produced magazines that actually showed people in the act of "making love" with pictures of bodies rotting in the sun, mutilated by the "wholesomeness of war" on opposite pages. With 60 pt. banners proclaiming, *"WHAT IS REALLY PORNOGRAPHIC?"* we sought to champion our own revolution.

The great thing about wanting something but not getting it is, it always seems great. But when you get that thing you thought would make your life complete, the thrill so soon wears off. We enter the stage that most of us sooner or later dwell in. It's called disillusionment. That's what began to happen to me. I had everything most men never get and I was depressed and unhappy most of the time. It's funny how influential music can be. When I was going through my *existentialist* metamorphosis I had Jimi telling me to live my life like I wanted to. Now I had B.B. convincing me that the thrill was gone.

It's My Life Let Me Live It Like I Want Too!

Sabu was quite a character. I never really liked him. He was a handsome figure of a young man who tooted his own horn way too much for me. He envisioned himself as God's gift to women and some sort of romantic "cat-burglar." Together we pulled off some incredible daytime and nighttime heists. I had dabbled in this arena before, and found it exciting. With the thrill gone out of my life this was just the "shot in the arm" I thought I needed.

We dealt in the commercial end of the business. For some distorted reason we felt that set us a grade above those who preyed on the less fortunate individuals who didn't own their own business. Thus we stayed away from residential capers. How ironic that a drug deal gone sour should end up in my going to prison for a residential burglary.

It was part of the deal. Through an interstate compact agreement, my home state agreed to supervise my parole period. The Jesus movement was in full swing and I had been corresponding with a girl who was telling me that Jesus was the only way. I guess it had affected me more than I knew. The stage was all prepared for my date with destiny.

A Date with Destiny
Chapter 10

Finally, back in the familiar surroundings of home I started getting bored again. It was then that I renewed riding Harleys and settling back into the old life-style.

The emptiness in me was me crying out to be filled. During this time, a couple who worked for the business I robbed, also lived in my home. They were running a covert operation for God—they were praying for me. Scott was the man who lived in my house. I knew he and Karen were Christians but the definition of what a Christian was was not clear in my mind.

Scott always seemed so happy or peaceful, so one day I asked him if he was taking a drug I had not heard of yet. I was not prepared for the answer he gave me.

"Yes, Jim, I take LJC every day."

"What the hell is LJC anyway? I never heard of that one," I bellowed.

"Jim," Scott said, "LJC stands for Lord Jesus Christ, and he is better than any drug you will ever take."

"Don't give me that Jesus stuff," I snapped back, "I've heard it all before. Christians are nothing but a bunch of hypocrites!"

"Jim, that may be partially true, but don't judge Jesus because we don't measure up to his standard of perfection," Scott replied.

What happened next, I can only describe as the divine intervention of God. As I was turning to go away to catch a buzz and go for a ride, I found myself spin on my heel and ask Scott when he and Karen were going to church again.

He quickly answered, "Tonight." I could hardly believe the next question that came out of my mouth.

"Scott, do you think it would be cool if I go?" I do not know who was the more surprised, him or me.

The rest of that day, I had the feeling that my life was going to change. I had a date with destiny and my destiny's name was Jesus Christ.

As I listened to the little gray-haired evangelist proclaim the Gospel, (the good news of God's love for me), it was better than a cold glass of spring water after a hot day in the desert. I had never heard anyone say that we had to accept Jesus as our Lord in order to get the benefits of His glorious salvation.

Ellen B., the Evangelist, said that simple acknowledgement that Jesus was as the Son of God was not good enough. The demons did that and trembled, but none of them would be saved or end up in heaven. You had to trust Him with your life.

The ride home found me in a daze. I did not know what was happening. It was as if time was suspended. The whole universe awaited the answer to some unasked question.

As I walked into the house Karen's queries as to what I thought of the service fell on deaf ears. Behind my bedroom door a force greater than anything I could have imagined was waiting for me.

A Date with Destiny

Many have suggested that what happened next might have been the result of residual hallucinogenic drugs in my blood stream. From time to time, I have wondered myself, but I do know one thing—my life has never been the same.

I closed the bedroom door behind me and was overwhelmed with what I now know was the presence of God. I started to cry. I asked Him to forgive me and accept my life without reservations.

I do not believe the ceiling in my bedroom actually disappeared, but it did seem to become transparent. I clearly saw the night sky. Then, as if in answer to my plea, the stars appeared, and transformed into the face of Jesus.

There was no audible conversation or dialogue, yet we communed together throughout night. What I remember most vividly was His eyes, not the physical aspect. Instead, what I saw inside His eyes. The external aspect of my awareness vanished, as I seemed to be drawn inside of Him.

In His incredible light, I felt His sorrow over my sin. I knew my sin had caused Him to suffer great pain.

However, I never felt any condemnation. He returned forgiveness and acceptance for my wickedness.

The majority of the time I spent in releasing my guilt to Him. I knew that He knew everything about me, but He seemed to want me to let Him see it all. It was as if my shame could cover my sin from His sight, but when I let Him see all the evil, guilt and pain, He was then able to take it away from me. This went on all night long and the continual weeping seemed more like a river of cleansing than a river of agony. Sometime in the early hours of the morning, I fell asleep for a brief time.

When I awoke, I felt as though I had awakened for the first time. I was so rested and full of peace. The joy that filled my heart had me literally doing cartwheels on the sidewalk that day! I felt like I was five years old and it was Christmas morning. I felt different. I knew what happened. I had become what Christians commonly call "Born-again."

St. Paul said that he had learned to be content, no matter what the situation. As I stood in front of the judge awaiting sentencing, I was preparing to find out exactly what he meant.

A Date with Destiny

"Mr. Golden, do you have anything to say before this court passes sentence on you?" I had rehearsed my speech repeatedly in my mind. I knew exactly what I wanted to say, but now that the moment of truth had arrived it seemed too melodramatic.

"Your honor, if I told you there are two forces in this world—good and evil—trying to gain control of our lives, you might think I am crazy. Therefore, I won't say that. I will say that when a person is under the influence of the drugs I was using, evil always has the upper hand. What I did was wrong and for that, I am deeply sorry. I have tried to make restitution and completed a drug and alcohol rehab course. Now I can do no more than throw myself on the mercy of the court."

As the final words dribbled down my chin, I braced myself for the worst.

"After reviewing your case history, as well as your pre-sentence investigation report from the parole department and your letters of reference, I sentence you to five years in the State Penal Facility in Hagerstown."

Some of my new Christian friends were sitting in the back of the courtroom praying. The judge's pronouncement released the cry,

"Jesus, O Lord Jesus, NO!"

"But," the judge continued, "I am going to suspend four and a half years of that and recommend you for the work release program."

Murmurs of "Thank you Jesus," and "Praise the Lord" filled the back of the courtroom.

"You are to be remanded to the Sheriff's custody and incarcerated at the Seven Locks County Correctional Facility until such time as a determination can be reached regarding your eligibility for the work release program. Your release and rehabilitation is in your hands. I wish you luck and hope you make the most of the opportunity before you. A great number of people have gone to bat for you."

It was 1972, I was twenty-four years old, a biker, and I had Jesus living in my heart—not as bad a combination as it might sound. One thing I always hated as a biker was social pretense. The main reason

I never continued to go to church from my youth was the hypocrisy I saw in those who did.

Hypocrisy is like alcoholism. It is a disease. Moreover, the ones who have this disease not only will not admit it, but also do not believe they have it in many cases. Hypocrisy is commonly defined as saying one thing and doing another but the religious hypocrite is one who claims to live and speak for Jesus, but wouldn't recognize Jesus if He was standing in front of them with a big name tag on His lapel.

Just think about it for a minute. Who did Jesus call hypocrites? It was the "devout" or "religious" leaders of His day. Scribes and Pharisees were at the top of the list. They claimed that they knew and served God. Yet, they were "Gods" self-appointed representatives.

The "religious" leaders were responsible for nailing Christ to the cross. One of the main reasons Jesus came was to restore each individual person to their Heavenly Father. Much of Christianity actually hinders this one-on-one relationship. It seeks to complicate our Christian lives, often making us feel we need someone "smart" enough or "anointed" enough to guide us in the right way. This subtly suggests that Jesus can't really do the job Himself.

If you are like I was, looking for what will fill that empty space inside, I will give you the words Scott gave to me. I am so glad I listened to them, and I hope you will too.

"Jim...don't judge Jesus because we don't measure up to His standard of perfection." Jesus loves you and wants to be your friend and Savior. The emptiness we all feel inside is shaped exactly like Jesus and nothing else can fill it!

If Jesus is speaking to your heart to let Him in, please do not turn your back on Him. Praying is talking, ask him to take charge of your life-then tell somebody what you have done and find others who have asked Jesus to be their Savior and Lord to hang out with.

Jesus & Jail!

Chapter 11

I did not want to leave you hanging. After I was reprimanded to the Sheriff's custody and incarcerated at Seven Locks Correctional Facility things went my way!

With Jesus as my constant companion, my stay in jail was like a paid vacation. I had never known such joy was possible. I couldn't have been happier if I had won a million dollar lottery. I immediately started taking bible study courses offered by the jail's chaplain. Two weeks before I was transferred to the "halfway house" work release program, everyone heard the story of my conversion, whether they wanted to or not! It isn't very often that you literally have a captive audience, 24 hours a day, seven days a week.

It was during this time that I met some Marion Brotherhood Monks who ministered in a number of prison facilities in the area. Later I would share my testimony and the Gospel in Lorton Prison and other correctional facilities, through their ministry, with stirring results. In those days no one had told me that there were any differences between Christians or churches. As a result I believed the church was simply all those in every place who call on the name of the Lord. I still feel the same way today, regardless of how things appear on the social surface!

Not too long after I moved from the "jailhouse" to the "halfway house" I met a man named Paul. Now "my" Paul wasn't anything like Jesus' Paul, as you will soon find out. He was a very large man whose simple-minded ways made him seem smaller than his true bulk. He was in jail for abusing one of his children. The exact nature and extent of the abuse was never really made clear to me but it was against his young son. Paul also had a small Mongoloid girl and two other daughters. His wife was a member of the Pentecostal Church of God that his younger daughter and son both attended.

During one of his family's visits, I met his older daughter, Kathy. She was a 17 year old "free spirit" who, though she was attractive, acted like the son

Paul wished he had had. Kathy was her father's right hand "man". Paul owned and operated his own small hauling business. It was actually more like a junk business because most of what he hauled away for other people he hauled into his house or backyard. At the time I was working for Rollins Park Shell. I had the "exalted" position of part time tow truck driver and gas pump "jockey."

When I first met the girl (Terry) I was going to marry, all I did was talk about her. I am certain I seized just about every opportunity I could to tell somebody about her. Fathers and mothers and grandparents do the same thing every time a new child is born. It is our nature, to talk about the things that excite us or the people we love. Now at this stage of my Christian walk, I was still infatuated with the one who saved my soul. I took advantage of every opportunity I had to tell everyone I met, towed or serviced at work, about my love for Jesus, come rain or shine. This evangelism, which I am sure could have been a little more tactful, was soon called to the attention of my employer.

John was a good old Baptist boy with the usual amount of vices. He smoked and drank on occasion.

Jesus & Jail

He cussed a little, looked at the women and was caught up into the material world a little too much from my perspective. But he went to church on Sunday and paid his tithe. What was in his heart I won't try to judge, but he tolerated my witnessing until he started losing business. That may be partially true. I did have a tendency to try and do the Holy Spirit's job of convicting people of what I considered inappropriate behavior. In my mind, the fact that John was my boss couldn't stop me from showing him the error of his ways. You notice I said DID have a tendency. It doesn't take God long to remind us that it's not by works of righteousness, which we have done, but according to his mercy he saved us.

This reminder started with me being fired from my job. Fortunately I had just completed my six-month stay in jail and was free to start living my life with minimal supervision. I soon found myself living with the mechanic from Rollins Park, his wife and baby girl. I had known Tommy B., through his wife's sister, Sherry. Laurie was the calmer of the two. Sherry and I had been party friends in the "old" days. Being associated with people that lived like I used to and going to work with Paul and his daughter Kathy set the stage for my first flirtation with real temptation and failure.

"Filthy Frank", as he was lovingly referred to by his "bros", was my closest friend in the biker scene. One night I had led him to the Lord and he told me how much better he felt. I had never felt such happiness for another human being in my life. Frank had found his God and Savior and I had been the instrument that introduced the two of them. However, the next day he started smoking PCP again and I started trying to be the voice of The Holy Spirit again. I thought that God delivered everybody just as he delivered me and that if he didn't; it was my job to make sure they delivered themselves! I suppose I had never realized what a miracle my instant deliverance from drugs was.

My pleas and exhortations did absolutely nothing for Frank, except drive him further and further away from me.

"Man, you're no fun to be around anymore!" was his farewell quote to me. We hardly saw each other for a year.

Jesus & Jail

It has been my experience that God's Word is true. Whatever a man plants he will harvest. I had been sowing seeds of pride and self-righteousness and within three months I would begin to reap a harvest. Sometime in the early period of my Christian life, I had a visit from an evil spirit. Naturally, I thought it was Satan. But the spirit never identified itself. It came into my room and looked like a beautiful woman at first. It was as "cool" as a Speilberg special effect and I was quite taken with it. Then, suddenly, its appearance began to alter and it turned into a hideous looking creature resembling a crouching old man. I felt as though it was ancient and evil beyond my wildest dreams and I froze with horror. I felt as if I were going to be crushed and suffocated at the same time. Then this creature began to masturbate in front of me and mingled with heinous laughter said, "You still have a few strokes left for me!"

When I felt as if I was just about to die, a little voice seemed to come from inside of me and it said only one word. I don't know if the word came as an audible sound or if it was only a thought, but not only did I hear it, but the spirit heard it as well. "Jesus," said the voice from within, three times. It seemed as though it got louder or stronger each time. The first time caused the spirit to withdraw to the corner of the room. The second time it howled with pain, as though struck with some invisible whip and it began to hover in the corner near the ceiling. The third time it was overwhelmed with shear terror and began to shake. It let out a scream that Scott and Karen heard in the next room and rocketed through the ceiling and out of sight. I slept for about 12 hours before I had enough strength to get up.

A few months or so after Frank said his farewell; this experience came back to mind, along with the "prophetic" message, "You still have a few strokes left for me!" For about the next six months or so, my spiritual life had more ups and downs than a roller coaster ride. I had all but returned to my old ways. I began using drugs, indulging in sexual immorality and partying for days at a time. But something was different. I had changed. I remember talking to Scott on the phone and telling him about the miserable state I was in. I hated the sin of my past but the deliverance that I had so easily experienced that night in my bedroom was nowhere to be found. It wasn't until God had taught me a little about his grace and delivering power that I learned not to take it for granted anymore. What I had taken for granted,

Jesus & Jail

God's precious Son had suffered and died to secure. I was learning to live in the forgiveness of Calvary.

Not Perfect, Just Forgiven!

Chapter 12

The bumper sticker read, "**Christians are not perfect, just forgiven!**" It was as if God was trying to get my attention. He was trying to lay a foundation in my life that could survive the storms of deceit and the winds of doctrine and bring me into an unbreakable relationship of total dependency on him. My mother used to say; "You should give credit where credit is due." Now my Heavenly Father was simply adding his Amen! New Years' resolutions never worked for me, before I was a Christian. I don't know what made me think that just because I was a Christian I could make them work for me now.

I think that my new found faith was being tested, not by me, but by God. It was not as if he needed to see if it was real, but he knew I needed to see it was. Some of my old "bros" had started coming around, telling me how slick a move I had put on everyone with the "born-again" scam I had run. I was starting to wonder if what they were saying was true. Yet deep down inside I knew I had been changed, even though many Christians might not have been convinced by the demonstration of my life.

After the phone conversation I had with Scott, I noticed that my heart began to slowly change again. I am not sure if it was my heart that was changing or if some type of spiritual "clutch" was being adjusted or rebuilt by the Spirit of God inside me. The engine in your car can be turning at 5000 rpm but if your clutch is blown or out of adjustment, your car will not go anywhere. The frustration I shared with Scott was over hating my sin and not being able to stop sinning. Whatever God was doing, it was causing my heart (engine) to transfer power to my mind (clutch) and drive my life (car) in the direction he and I really wanted to go.

Every good mechanic always test drives a car he has repaired in order to fine tune and test his repair work to be certain he has corrected the problem. In a sense, God is the same way. He will perfect that which concerns each one of us. It seemed that he wanted to make sure I knew whom salvation belonged to. He had started a "good work" of salvation in me, and he didn't want me messing it up. A constant reminder of my inability to save myself was all the help God wanted or needed from me.

Things had been going fairly well. I had begun to attend a big teaching meeting, in a local high school, called T.A.G. Two young men named Larry and C.J. taught there. Things were exciting and the meetings were growing by leaps and bounds. Their practical method of applying scriptural truths, mixed with humorous anecdotes and meaningful contemporary illustrations soon gained them a large following. They were the "talk of the town." Pastors began to entrust their youth to these young men's tutelage every Tuesday night. Soon they outgrew the Maryland meeting places available to them and Pastor "Mac" opened up his 2000 person capacity church building to them for the Tuesday night meeting. It was located in the N.W. section of Washington, D.C., and because it was more accessible it wasn't long before near capacity crowds began to gather weekly.

I was in regular attendance and even ministered in the "healing room" with a young Korean man named Ché.

Not Perfect, Just Forgiven!

From time to time I ministered to those desiring to receive the "baptism" of the Holy Spirit as well. I had become very proud of my spiritual prowess and stability. It was, however, just about time for God to take me on a road test.

Let no man say when he is tempted he is tempted by God...but he is rather drawn away by his own lust and enticed. God isn't the tempter. He is the controller of our lust, when and if we will acknowledge that we are just like any other man without his protecting and enabling fruit of self-control.

It seemed that overnight I had this incredible desire to find my old friend Frank. I had made new friends but most of the relationships were more tutorial in nature. I was either teacher or student and there was very little "friendship" as I understood it.

"Hey, man, long time no see. How are things going?" Frank seemed surprised to see me again and while I suspected God had a much deeper plan than He was willing to let me in on, I could see in Frank's eyes the need to be with an old friend. "When did you get that new car bro?" Frank questioned. "About a month ago, want to take a ride?" "Sure, man, I need to go out to

Olney. Have you got enough time?" Frank asked. "No problem, hop in."

As we drove out Georgia Avenue, he told me how the gang wars had affected his life. He had his beautiful "show" scooter (motorcycle) stolen and two members of a rival gang, at gunpoint, made him sign the title over to them. They threatened to kill him and rape and beat his old lady if he called the police. We both knew they were not making idle threats and anyway, he would never see his scooter again. Frank B. had finally had his fill of the wild life for a while. As we drove along talking, I shared some of my frustrations as well. Neither of us was offering advise to the other, we were simply sharing each other's pain. The next thing I knew he had a joint (marijuana) out and we were getting high.

This didn't just happen "overnight", in all truthfulness. I had recently been entertaining thoughts about getting high. Even though I had thought of myself as being spiritually mature and stable because of my involvement with T.A.G. and my living in a household with Ché, the joy of God's salvation had slowly started disappearing again.

Not Perfect, Just Forgiven!

As we drove down the road I suddenly felt like someone who just got caught cheating on his wife. In that instant I knew how much my sin was hurting God. It wasn't the act of smoking pot that hurt him; it was my trying to find fulfillment in something other than him. Suddenly, it hit home. Christianity wasn't a religious philosophy. It was a marriage union between God and man. I was no longer to seek my gratification or fulfillment from any source but him.

The next pass of the joint found me telling Frank no, thank you, and letting him know that I felt like I was cheating on my beautiful wife (Jesus) with some "old hag" (the joint). It just was not worth it.

"Jim, I don't know what's going on with you, man, one minute you're smokin' dope and enjoying the buzz just like old times. The next minute you're spouting all this sanctimonious Christian crap. Man, I think Christians ought to admit that they're just a bunch of hypocrites!"

"No, Frank, that's not it. Christians aren't perfect, just forgiven!"

NOTE: **SIGNIFICANT LIVES,** installment two of Jim's autobiography begins where this book stops, and covers over two decades of Jim's life as a Christian. It is a book born out of the struggles and frustrations of being a Christian, as well as a leader in the 21st century Charismatic Church.

www.ingramcontent.com/pod-product-compliance
Lightning Source LLC
Chambersburg PA
CBHW071734040426
42446CB00012B/2357